# SMALL PLEASURES

by
Nikia Leopold

Blue Light Press

*Winner of the 2012 Blue Light Poetry Prize*
**SMALL PLEASURES**
Copyright 2021 By Nikia Leopold

All rights reserved. Printed in the United States of America. No part of this book may be used or reproduced in any manner without written permission except in the case of brief quotations embodied in critical articles and reviews.

BLUE LIGHT PRESS
www.bluelightpress.com
bluelightpress@aol.com

1ST WORLD PUBLISHING
PO Box 2211
Fairfield, IA 52556
www.1stworldpublishing.com

BOOK & COVER DESIGN
Melanie Gendron
melaniegendron999@gmail.com

COVER ART:
Nikia Leopold

AUTHOR PHOTO:
Bruce Leopold

FIRST PRINTING: 2012

SECOND PRINTING: 2021

ISBN: 1-886361-26-6

## Acknowledgments

My grateful acknowledgments to the editors of publications in which some of these poems appeared or are forthcoming:

*The American Scholar:* "Belief;" "Morning"
*The Baltimore Review:* "Paper White Narcissi"
*The Baltimore Sun:* "Uncertain Spring"
*The Bitter Oleander:* "October Fog"
*The Christian Science Monitor:* "Risotto;" "Vowels"
*Green Mountains Review:* "Oblique;" "Plague Weather;" "Thirst"
*Passager:* "Quicken;" "Small Pleasures;" "Woodpeckers"
*Poet Lore:* "Pool"
*Poetry East:* "The Beach Glass;" "Lilac;" "The Red Tulips"

"Morning" appeared in the Anthology of Magazine Verse & Yearbook of American Poetry: 1997 edition.

"Small Pleasures" appeared in *Burning Bright: Passager Celebrates 21 Years* (Passager Books, 2011.)

"The Beach Glass" was included in *Wider than the Sky: Thirty Years of Poetry East.* (2011.)

Some of these poems were published in a chapbook, *Dark Feathers,* by Finishing Line Press, 2004.

## Contents

| | |
|---|---|
| Morning | 1 |
| Lilac | 2 |
| Woodpeckers | 3 |
| The Button Shop | 4 |
| Oblique | 5 |
| Spinning to Fall | 6 |
| Pool | 7 |
| October Fog | 8 |
| Plague Weather | 9 |
| Quicken | 10 |
| Belief | 11 |
| Paper White Narcissi | 12 |
| Blur | 13 |
| Uncertain Spring | 14 |
| Small Pleasures | 15 |
| Vowels | 16 |
| Risotto | 17 |
| The Red Tulips | 18 |
| Thirst | 19 |
| Magic | 20 |
| Vector | 21 |
| Invisible | 22 |
| The Beach Glass | 23 |
| About the Author | 25 |

# SMALL PLEASURES

For Bruce

**Morning**

Dawn slips through cracks
made by branches,
through slits of birdcalls.
Dreams burn off,
rising from quiet houses
like steam.
The paper lands
on each walk
with a flat slap
of facts,
and we wake once more,
sense the body's
precious oils and salts,
stretch and stand,
grateful even for the stiffness
that roots us
to this day.

## Lilac

Miss Kim is in delectable bloom.
The lucent white of her flowers
hints of asphodel.
How tender her breath.
My father, who loved
the feminine, would be
well pleased to know that
her maiden roots caress his ashes.

## Woodpeckers

Because I chose to have no children,
there will be no burial,
no scattering.
When my skeleton is clean
hang it in a cherry tree,
legacy of long light bones
making music with the wind,
drumming to the 'tock' of woodpeckers
on a hollow trunk.
I hope the neighbors will listen
to my knocking with some pleasure
and no fear —
I've never really wanted to come in.

**The Button Shop**

is an aisle
lined by drawers,
each compartment
holding reliquaries
of pierced bone,
pearl, and porcelain.
I sooth my fingers
among smooth disks
of coconut shell,
like the ones on
my old aloha shirt—
from that time when
we were new and you
slipped the buttons free
as we held our breath,
air quivering around us.

**Oblique**

There are times
when the only way to find
a hummingbird is by the agitation
of a morning glory's heaven,
when a lily pad's shudder
hints at fish,
and one green swath betrays
a river sunken in the cropped field —
times when grass is bleached by sun
and only shadows let me guess
the depth of roots.
When he is silent, distant,
hidden as a tree-lined stream,
I've learned that to find him
I must turn slightly from him,
speak of anything,
but what is between us.

**Spinning to Fall**

Evenings are sly
after the solstice,
lingering, caressing
basil, cherry tomatoes,
tricking us into believing
the light will last,
conjuring a longer day—
more time to weed
or reconcile
before sleep.
But the festival is over,
the star is bowing out,
life leaches subtly from
apricots, plums, stone fruit
dropping like sweet flesh.

**Pool**

Leaves drift into the empty
swimming pool tonight,
collect at the juncture
of shallow and deep.
I walk to the taut
end of the diving board,
and within its slight
reverberation, gauge the catch,
watch the magnified
tesserae, raw aqua,
that line this
inverted mausoleum.

**October Fog**

Leaves strain
through a sieve of white mist.
The windshield is milk glass.

I slow down, open the windows
and forest drifts in —
damp bark, moss, coolness —

a poultice for that old grievance
I woke with, which stops burning,
turns to vapor,
slips between maples
like the ghost of a fox.

**Plague Weather**

Warm November,
mist of fruit flies
over the pears,
renaissance of moths
flying again
to fiery deaths
in votives.

Burn on a wrist
turns to itself,
mending.

A neighbor has died
of lung cancer.

The body reawakens
to desire, then
desires its end . . .
Mind closes its eyes,
afraid of fire.

Each day a breath
taken in,
expelled, fragile
as onionskin.

## Quicken

My father has forgotten old friends,
but remembers fireworks we watched
three months ago, he in his wheelchair,
I next to him, an arm around his slender
shoulders, feeling them tense
with each ecstasy of rockets.

Now he asks, "That night . . . weren't
those flowers in the sky?"
I put down the spoon.
This man of ninety-two, stripped slowly
of so much, can quicken sparks
to petals, flesh them into bloom.

## Belief

The pine, grown to be cut,
tilts in its bucket,
untrimmed, drawing water
through the stub of trunk.
I'm surprised by its fragrance —
its silent breath — reminded
that breathing is steady luck,
a constant surprise,
and I too, stand between
floor and ceiling, cut
from belief in anything but
the presence of dark boughs
and the hope of something gleaming.

**Paper White Narcissi**

Cloistered in a blue bowl,
they meditate in darkness,

fast on winter light and water.
Roots say pebble rosaries.

Pale shoots become a green choir
surging to the window.

Slender throats swell with pearls,
burst at last in tiny white hosannas

praising their reflection on cold glass,
their sacrifice to conjure spring in winter,

each cluster echoing her sisters'
thin sweet incense on the air.

**Blur**

I can't tell anymore
if the snow is coming
from the sky
or is lifted by the wind.
Either way it's
a fierce partisan
of no partitions,
and while I admire
its democracy
what I love
is the way
it locks us alone
in our own kingdom.

## Uncertain Spring

After difficult labor
winter is finally
delivered
of snowdrops,
pale and small,
close to the earth,
as the newborn cub
of a polar bear,
long waited for,
its life uncertain,
clutched to its mother's
vast white breast,
all the green shoots
urging its breath.

**Small Pleasures**


An egg spills double yolks into the pan.
The watering can is heavy, filled already.
That bracelet he gave me reappears —
turquoise seam between floorboards.
A wren darts into the kitchen and out again.
The tiny death-rattle of a burnt-out light bulb.
Those instants when the full moon
seems to shift from disc to sphere . . .
Pleasures with the heft of tinsel,
so small they're irreducible.

**Vowels**

Lovely luxuries,
breathy
starlets of the alphabet.

**Risotto**

Beyond the kitchen window
white limbs of sycamore
are swimming in the wind.
Threads of saffron stain
the grains of rice with pollen.
Stirring, I think of Leopardi's sweet
shipwreck in the depths of time and eternity.
My wooden spoon's the present to be licked,
the distant tree infinity to worship.

## The Red Tulips

are dying, stems
twisting north, south,
petal-mouths moaning
silently
from their vase
as we lunch
above them, unmindful
that our own deaths
are poised, sure
as splayed leaves,
as fruit-flies drowning
in wine, as shadows
bruising every angle
of the afternoon.

**Thirst**

The marigold has grown
so dense with leaves
and pungent blossoms
that rain glances from it,
missing the glazed pot, and now,
in the midst of downpour, the roots
know drought, the flowers wilt,
the way we extend ourselves,
obscuring our deepest needs,
sleeping without dreams,
growing cover that kills.

## Magic

Light years ago,
my father set out cones,
fountains, rockets, on our parched lawn.
His was the box of matches.
The first time he
deemed me old enough
he tossed them to me, saying,
"Light 'em and run!"
Mother cried, "Not yet!"
Amid the jetting jewels,
the spray of crystals, geysers
of violet sparks,
I never felt the pain.
I breathed deep of gunpowder,
my hand fell into my father's,
who let me make magic.
My thumb still bears the scar.

**Vector**

A hummingbird's
flight
is all angles,
strict, precise,
tongue piercing
a trumpet flower
with nun-like
purity of purpose,
rejecting everything
but sips
of nectar
petaled in red —
rigid angel of delight.

**Invisible**

The changes happen slowly,
marking the girl,
the woman:
wrinkles, lax flesh,
waning muscle, each line
erasing her until
she becomes invisible
padding on the silk
where ocean meets sand,
no flat abdomen
attracting attention,
vanity leached away,
just herself, alert
for bright bits of shell.

**The Beach Glass**

sleeps in my palm,
quietly shining through
its gentle sugar,
pale green of skies
lit by circuses.

To grow beautiful
and useless with the years,
to glow in your hands.

# About the Author

Niki Leopold is a graduate of the Johns Hopkins Writing Seminars in Poetry, and has a Ph.D. in Art History, also from Hopkins. Her poems have appeared in *The American Scholar, Commonweal, Poetry East* and *Poetry*. Finishing Line Press published her chapbook, *Dark Feathers*. Her children's book, *Adam's Crayons*, is out from Galileo Press. She lives with her husband in Ruxton, Maryland.

www.ingramcontent.com/pod-product-compliance
Lightning Source LLC
Chambersburg PA
CBHW032005060426
42449CB00031B/807